IMAGES OF

INDUSTRIAL & NARROW GAUGE RAILWAYS - DEVON

IMAGES OF

INDUSTRIAL & NARROW GAUGE RAILWAYS - DEVON

CLASSIC PHOTOGRAPHS FROM
THE MAURICE DART RAILWAY COLLECTION

HALSGROVE

First published in Great Britain in 2010

British Library Cataloguing-in-Publication Data
A CIP record for this title is available from the British Library

ISBN 978 1 84114 860 1

Halsgrove
Halsgrove House,
Ryelands Industrial Estate,
Bagley Road, Wellington, Somerset TA21 9PZ
Tel: 01823 653777   Fax: 01823 216796
email: sales@halsgrove.com

Part of the Halsgrove group of companies
Information on all Halsgrove titles is available at: www.halsgrove.com

Printed and bound in Great Britain by Cromwell Press Group., Wiltshire

CONTENTS

INTRODUCTION

At a very early age I was taken to Dockyard Halt, near Devonport and following a move, to St Budeaux stations to 'watch trains'. I was taught to remember the names of three engines that passed through. At home there was a Hornby Gauge '0' model railway. Most Saturday afternoons my parents would take me with them from St Budeaux to either Devonport, reached by tram, or Plymouth, to which we caught a 'motor train' to Millbay. So my interest in railways steadily developed. During the summers of 1937, 1938 and 1939, the three of us spent a week travelling by train to Torquay, Paignton or Goodrington, with sometimes a venture to Kingswear and across to Dartmouth on the 'MEW' or to Dawlish Warren. We used a family holiday runabout ticket for the week and set out from St Budeaux on an excursion train that ran daily from Saltash to Paignton and which, from memory, was usually hauled by a Castle class locomotive to Newton Abbot. From our front windows at Higher St Budeaux I was able to watch trains in the distance as they climbed towards the Devon side of the Royal Albert Bridge. They could also be seen as they rounded the curves west of Saltash station. I asked my father on one occasion why we did not go to Cornwall instead of to Paignton and he replied that it was better to go up the line. This was probably because there was a daily excursion train from Saltash to Paignton although we frequently had to change trains at Newton Abbot and cross over the footbridge. My father would bring home books about railways. They had been loaned to him for me to look at and contained many photographs of railway subjects. During the Second World War, following the second batch of blitz raids on Plymouth when many schools were damaged, I was evacuated to Bude by train from Friary. I stood in the corridor for most of the way to "see where I was going" much to the consternation of the WVS ladies who were accompanying us. I recall seeing a tank engine, at what I later learned was Meldon Quarry, carrying 500S on its tank side. This was the T class 'Service loco'. Whilst at Bude I began to hear about places such as Holsworthy and Okehampton, which I had passed through on the train. Evacuation to Bude was followed by a short period back at St Budeaux after which I spent two years at St Austell, using trains to and from North Road. Whilst there, at the evacuated Grammar school, I met many older boys who were railway enthusiasts and my 'railway education' commenced properly. I also had my first sight of an Industrial locomotive as the train passed Par Harbour.

My father had been transferred from Devonport to the Dockyard at Gibraltar during 1944, and in the summer of 1947 I went there by sea for a holiday for several weeks. My father was an amateur photographer and whilst there he taught me to use a box camera. I immediately started taking photographs of Gibraltar Dockyard locomotives from a balcony! I began to appreciate the variety of different types of Industrial locomotives that were to be seen. On returning to St Budeaux I found my father's two old cameras and managed to obtain a film for each. A large folding Kodak that used A-122 film turned out to have a pin hole in the bellows, only discovered when the results of the first film were seen. This made it unusable. The other was an old Box Brownie which had a push-over lever shutter release and had one good and one faulty viewfinder that showed two images, one above the other. I persevered with this but did not know enough to achieve much success. I tried to record trains passing through St Budeaux and went to Laira shed late in September and took photos, some against the low evening sun. Still, we all had to learn by experience. With those which I had taken at Gibraltar, this was the start of my collection of railway photographs. My employment commenced at Lee Moor so I became conversant with the Lee Moor Tramway and its two locomotives. I had previously seen the bottom end of the tramway before war had broken out when visiting relations who lived at Laira Wharf. On those visits I was always taken across to the stables to see the horses which worked trains on the lower section of the line. Later, my employment took me to lodge at St Austell where I finally took up permanent residence. As time progressed I was able to buy better cameras and commenced longer railway trips to places further afield. My railway interest widened from purely collecting engine names and numbers to encompass signalling and railway history. This was progressed by meeting more very knowledgeable older railway enthusiasts and railwaymen, many of whom became lifelong friends of mine. I developed a desire to obtain photographs of some of the locomotives that I had seen in my early years, so the process of searching for and purchasing photos commenced. As my interest and knowledge grew, so likewise did the quest for more photos. This now encompassed all of Devon and Cornwall and large sections of Wales, along with various classes of locomotives from all over the country. An interest in Narrow Gauge and Industrial Railways developed. So the 'Archive' steadily grew from filling an expanding suitcase to occupying a considerable expanse of shelf space in two rooms.

When it was suggested that I compile some books making use of some of these images I thought that it would be a great idea as many of them, to the best of my knowledge, had not previously been used in publications.

Previous books covered mainly the main line railway companies in the West and South of England, with a companion volume to this covering Cornwall. With so many photos available the choice has been difficult but constraints such as copyright and previous use have been considered. Also as many standard gauge industrial steam and diesel locos are preserved these are mainly not included. This includes those which have been or are at the Plym Valley Railway, the South Devon Railway and the Paignton & Dartmouth Railway. This is not an attempt to include every location in the area or all types of locomotive that have worked here but is simply a selection from my collection. Industrial lines came in a great variety of gauges and motive power ranged from manual and horse power to steam, diesel and even electric propulsion. This book is not intended to provide a history of the various systems included as most of these are well documented in other publications. The locations are laid out alphabetically in groups of industries which correspond to the order in which they are filed in my collection. A location index is included at the end of the photographs. Some older not photographically perfect images are included because of their historic value and interest. I have attempted to give a good coverage of a variety of lines and motive power in Cornwall from the mid 1900s to the present day. These images may be of great interest to modellers of industrial locations and railways. Not all of the photos portray locomotives and a few of them will require close examination to locate sections of rail on long abandoned lines. When exploring these old lines finds such as lengths of rail cause much excitement and a feeling of great satisfaction.

As this book features images from my personal collection, the layout follows the order in which the collection is arranged in twelve groups covering different sections of industry and longer lines. Readers seeking photos at specific locations should refer to the index at the end of the book. I have attempted to make the captions detailed without delving too deeply into railway history or becoming too technical. Readers seeking further information on some of these lines should consult the Reference section. Any errors that are discovered are purely attributable to myself. I trust that within the contents there is material to cater for most railway interests and that memories of a bygone age of railways will be recalled.

ACKNOWLEDGEMENTS

I express special thanks to my friend of many years, Mike Daly and also Kenneth Brown and Roger Hateley, also to the Stephenson Locomotive Society for permission to reproduce photos taken by them or in their collections. Also my thanks and apologies are proffered to other photographers whose work has been used and not credited. My thanks are also proffered to the management and staff at the re-opened Lynton & Barnstaple Railway and Morwellham Quay. I also extend my thanks and gratitude to the owners and staff at the Exmoor Steam Railway, the Devon Railway Centre, Bere Ferrers, Christow and Bicton Woodland Railway for access and opportunities for photography. Likewise I extend my sincere thanks to Colonel Clark, Commandant of Okehampton Camp and other Dartmoor Ranges for access and information. Where no credit is given the photographer is unknown. I am also indebted to Simon Butler of Halsgrove for suggesting the idea of this series of books.

REFERENCE SOURCES

A Historical Survey Of The Mines & Mineral Railways of East Cornwall & West Devon. D.B. Barton. D. Bradford Barton.

Branch Line To Lynton. Vic Mitchell & Keith Smith. Middleton Press.

British Narrow Gauge Steam. Michael Messenger. D. Bradford Barton.

Cliffhangers. Michael J. Burrell. Pear Tree Cottage Publications.

Crossing's Dartmoor Worker. Brian Le Messurier ed., David & Charles.

Dartmoor. R.Hansford Worth. Richard Hansford Worth Estate.

Dartmoor. A New Study. Crispin Gill. David & Charles.

Dartmoor Railway. Past, Present & Future. John Hummel & David Payne. Dartmoor Railway.

Devonport Dockyard Railway. Paul Burkhalter.

Devon Narrow Gauge. Maurice Dart. Middleton Press.

From Haldon To Mid-Dartmoor in Old Photographs. Tim Hall. Alan Sutton Publishing.

Industrial Archaeology of Dartmoor. Helen Harris. David & Charles.

Industrial Archaeology of The Tamar Valley. Frank Booker. David & Charles.

Industrial Locomotives of South West England. Roger Hateley. Industrial Railway Society.

Industrial Railways of the South West. Michael Messenger. Twelveheads Press.

Light Railway Handbooks. Various editions. Oakwood Press.

Lundy. A & M. Langham. David & Charles.

Lundy Island. A Monograph. (1877) John R. Chanter. Cassel, Petter & Galpin.

Lynton & Barnstaple Railway Album. J.D.C. Prideaux. David & Charles.

Mineral Railways of the West Country. Tony Fairclough & Eric Shepherd. D.Bradford Barton.

Mines of Cornwall and Devon. Peter Stanier. Twelveheads Press.

Minor Railways. Peter Scott. Branch Line Society.

More British Narrow Gauge Steam. Michael Messenger. D.Bradford Barton.

North Devon Clay. Michael Messenger. Twelveheads Press.

One Man's Moor. William D.Lethbridge. Halsgrove.

Quarries of England & Wales. Peter Stanier. Twelveheads Press.

Stone Blocks and Iron Rails (Tramroads). Bertram Baxter. David & Charles.

The Bicton Woodland Railway. N.D.G. James. Rolle Estate Office.

The Bideford, Westward Ho! & Appledore Railway. Rod Garner. Kestrel Railway Books.

The Haytor Granite Tramway & Stover Canal. M.C. Ewans. David & Charles.

The Island of Lundy. A.F.Langham. Alan Sutton Publishing.

The Lee Moor Tramway. R.M.S. Hall. Oakwood Press.

The Lee Moor Tramway. Bryan Gibson. Plymouth Railway Circle.

The Lee Moor Tramway. A Pictorial Record. Roy E.Taylor. Twelveheads Press.

The Lundy Granite Company. Peter Rothwell & Myrtle Ternstrom. Westwell Publishing.

The Lynton & Barnstaple Railway. G.A. Brown, J.D.C. Prideaux & H.G. Radcliffe.

The Lynton & Barnstaple Railway. Yesterday & Today. P.Gower, B,Gray & K.Vingoe.

The Plymouth & Dartmoor Railway. H.G.Kendall. Oakwood Press.

The Redlake Tramway & China Clay Works. E.A. Wade. Twelveheads Press.

The Torrington & Marland Light Railway. Rod Garner. Kestrel Railway Books.

Thurlow's Dartmoor Companion. George Thurlow. Peninsula Press.

Walking The Dartmoor Railroads. Eric Hemery. Peninsula Press.

The author's collection of notes and articles on Devon's Industrial and Narrow Gauge lines.

The author's personal notebooks dating from 1945.

1

LYNTON & BARNSTAPLE RAILWAY (ORIGINAL)

This first section covers the 19 mile long 1ft 11½in gauge line which operated from 1898 until 1935. The line's history is well documented in various publications.

We commence with the last loco which the line obtained. 2-6-2T 188 'LEW' (MW 2042/1925) is outside the railway's Works, loco and carriage sheds at Pilton Yard, Barnstaple in the early 1930s. In 1936 this engine moved to an unknown location from where it is reputed to have been shipped to South America.

In the early 1920s before the SR absorbed the line 2-6-2T 'YEO' (MW 1361/1897) which became SR 759 is outside Pilton Yard loco shed. Photomatic.

Carrying SR livery 2-6-2T 759 'YEO' (MW 1361/1897) is outside Pilton Yard sheds on 24 May 1932.

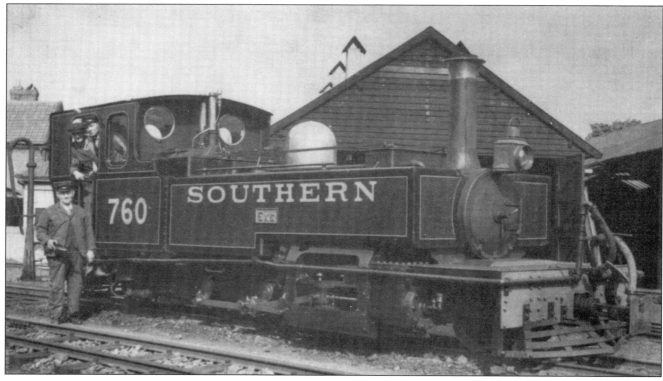

2-6-2T 760 'EXE' (MW 1362/1897) is at Pilton Yard in the early 1930s. Reginald T.Reeves.
Exmoor Heritage Postcards.

In the early 1920s 2-6-2T 'TAW' (MW 1363/1897) is receiving attention inside Pilton Yard Works. This loco became SR 761.

In the late 1920s 2-6-2T E761 'TAW' (MW 1363/1897) waits to depart from Barnstaple Town with a mixed train. The SR line from Barnstaple Junction to Ilfracombe is on the right.

An American loco built at the Baldwin Locomotive Works was obtained by the railway. 2-4-2T 'LYN' (BLW 15965/1898) is at Pilton Yard in the early 1920s. This loco became SR 762.

In SR livery 2-4-2T E762 'LYN' (BLW 15965/1898) is at Pilton Yard in the early 1930s.

Empty and loaded wagons stand in the loop at Woody Bay station in the early 1920s.
Locomotive & General Railway Photographs

In the early 1920s 2-6-2T 'YEO' (MW 1361/1897) waits to depart from Lynton.

The church forms a backdrop to the trackless station at Parracombe in the late 1940s. This view looks towards Lynton. Note the postbox affixed to the waiting shelter. The shelter was extant in 2009. Kenneth Brown.

In the early 1930s 2-6-2T E761 'TAW' (MW 1363/1897) waits at Blackmoor station with a mixed train to Barnstaple Town. The building with an extension added is now the Old Station House Inn.
J.Broom. Hotel & Restaurant.

2-6-2T 188 'LEW' (MW 2042/1925) is at Bratton Fleming with a mixed train for Barnstaple Town in the early 1930s.
Pamlin Prints.

With the station at its east end the stone Chelfham viaduct spans the valley in the early 1930s. This structure has been restored and is ready to receive track again.
Lynton Railway Station

This is Snapper Halt in the late 1920s with its tiny waiting shelter, low platform and approach path. Part of the shelter is extant.

In the late 1920s 2-6-2T 759 'YEO' (MW1361/1897) is at Barnstaple Town on a goods train for Lynton

In the early 1930s 2-6-2T E760 'EXE' (MW 1362/1897) is signalled to depart from Barnstaple Town with a train to Lynton. The L & B Goods shed and yard is in the mid-distance.

2

PLYMOUTH & DARTMOOR RAILWAY, LEE MOOR TRAMWAY

This section covers the south-west section of the early horse-worked 4ft 6in gauge P & D Rly which ran from Sutton Pool, Plymouth via Roborough and Yelverton to Princetown. Branch lines ran east to Marsh Mills, and Plympton. A further branch line ran to Cann Quarry. The Lee Moor Tramway started as a branch line off the Cann Quarry branch line from Plym Bridge and ran via two rope-worked inclines to Lee Moor village and its associated China Clay works. A further branch line ran west from Lee Moor Village to Wotter. At Plymouth the LMT diverged from the P & D's route and terminated at Laira Wharf. The complex history of these fascinating lines is well documented in other publications.

We start with an overview of the LMT's terminus at Laira Wharf in the 1930s taken from Laira Bridge which crosses the River Plym. Two rakes of wagons await unloading into ships. In the centre background is the Power station with its twin stacks. The clay company's house is below the stacks. The stables were to the right of the Power station. Various storage sheds are to the right of the house. The SR Cattewater branch is in front of the Power station and behind the clay company's buildings. Arthur Bray.

China Clay was shipped either as loose lumps (bulk clay) or in wooden casks. Loaded casks are being transferred from LMT wagons to a ship at Laira Wharf in the early 1920s.

English China Clays.

The LMT crossed SR lines once and GWR lines four times on the level. The LMT curved away past the back of the clay company's buildings and immediately crossed the SR's Cattewater branch just before both lines passed below Laira Bridge Road. This is the crossing and bridge in 1955 after the LMT had closed. Note the extension to the bridge due to road widening and the steep flight of access steps. The truncated line turned sharply left into a cutting to serve Pethick's Yard and once linked up with the GWR's Sutton Harbour branch.

Roy Sambourne/Transport Treasury.

In 1955 we look back through Laira Bridge Road bridge with its extension towards Laira Wharf. The LMT is on the right and part of a signal box is on the left. Roy Sambourne/Transport Treasury.

Beyond the bridge the two lines diverge as seen in this view from the 1930s. A loaded three-wagon LMT train hauled by two horses heads for Laira Wharf. The driver is almost hidden by the loaded wagons. The SR line is curving right and climbing to Cattewater Junction to join the Turnchapel and Yealmpton line descending from Laira Bridge.

The LMT line curves away from the Cattewater branch and approaches the GWR's Sutton Harbour branch. In this 1955 photo both lines have passed under Embankment Road. The Sutton Harbour branch on the right was originally the route of the P & D Rly to Sutton Pool. Roy Sambourne.

The Sutton Harbour branch joined the SR main line at Friary Junction and the LMT ran parallel to them. The four wagon two horse power LMT train has crossed the GWR's No.2 Spur from Cattewater Junction at Mount Gould Junction around 1930. Stephenson Locomotive Society.

From Mount Gould Junction the LMT ran on the east side of Laira Marshalling Yard where there were exchange sidings. On 6 July 1958 two LMT Crane wagons are on the exchange sidings. Maurice Dart.

This is the east end of Laira Yard in the 1930s. Nearest to the camera are LMT wagons loaded with bulk clay. The next two lines contain wagons loaded with coal bound for China Clay kilns. On the line behind the 'Toad' Brake van are GWR open wagons loaded with China Clay, probably from Marsh Mills kilns bound for Victoria Wharves at the end of the Cattewater branch. F.H.C. Casbourne/Stephenson Locomotive Society

A LMT train of three empty wagons and one loaded with coal drawn by two horses is crossing the GWR main lines at Laira Junction in the 1930s. The LMT driver is seated on the corner of the leading wagon. Boards were laid between the rails on the crossing for the benefit of the horses. Laira box is on the left with Laira shed in the upper left distance. Auto Car sidings are on the right. Note the one gate over the Up line. The gate closed the tramway route completely.

Four loaded LMT wagons drawn by two horses have passed under Embankment Road and approach Laira Crossing in the 1920s. The photographer appears to be attracting attention. Pamlin Prints.

The LMT skirted the River Plym and turned west towards Crabtree. There was a siding to hold three wagons off the long straight section approaching Crabtree which was recorded in the 1950s. English China Clays.

At Crabtree, adjacent to the Rising Sun Public House, the LMT crossed the main road from Plymouth to Plympton. This is the crossing in the early 1950s looking towards Marsh Mills. English China Clays.

At the end of Crabtree road crossing the LMT curved right. The original P&DR trackbed which continued straight ahead is shown in June 1953 with many granite setts to be seen. Maurice Dart.

From Crabtree after some distance the P&DR crossed Forder Valley Road and ran through woodland to a cutting leading to the 600yd Leigham (Cann) tunnel. This is the south portal of the tunnel on 14 April 1993. The tunnel is dead straight and has a headroom of 9ft 6in. There are several shafts. During the war it was used as an Air Raid Shelter since when it was used by the Plymouth City Council as a store. It is now securely bolted out of use.

Maurice Dart/Transport Treasury.

This is the north portal of Leigham tunnel in June 1953.
Denis Richards.

From the tunnel the P&DR skirted Plym Bridge Road and swung away north-west heading for Roborough. This is the start of that section containing many granite setts on 14 April 1993.
Maurice Dart/Transport Treasury.

The P&DR climbed and curved on its way from Leigham tunnel and crossed the road from Plym Bridge to Roborough. This is the abutments of the underline bridge in 1926. Stephenson Locomotive Society.

Returning to the route taken by the LMT from Crabtree the line crossed Forder Valley Road and then went over the much narrower River Plym. This is the bridge over the river on 14 October 1961. The bridge is still extant with rails laid and can be crossed by pedestrians.

At Marsh Mills the LMT crossed the short GWR branch line into MOD Coypool Depot and ran alongside the Tavistock branch line. This is that section approaching Plym Bridge in 1922. Note the granite setts on the right which had been replaced with wooden sleepers. F.H.C.Casbourne/Stephenson Locomotive Society.

On 12 March 1954 4500 class 2-6-2T 4530 approaches Lee Moor Crossing, south of Plym Bridge with a train from Launceston to Plymouth North Road. The loco appears to have tree branches laid across the buffer beam. The signal box is on the left. Larry Crosier.

This is Lee Moor Crossing looking south in 1922. The LMT siding on the left could have been laid to facilitate loading of one of the LMT locos onto a standard gauge wagon for transport to the Peckett Works at Bristol for overhaul. Or could it have been used by the Forestry Commission for loading trees for timber during the First World War. F.H.C. Casbourn/Stephenson Locomotive Society.

At Plym Bridge the P&DR Cann Quarry branch trackbed diverged north, crossed the road from Plym Bridge to Plympton and passed under the GWR's Tavistock branch from where it skirted the bank of the Cann Quarry Canal which it had replaced. On 28 June 1959 this looks south along the trackbed with many granite setts to be seen. The canal, which still contains water is on the left.

Maurice Dart/Transport Treasury.

A short distance above Lee Moor Crossing the foot of the cable worked Cann Wood Incline is reached where horses were attached and detached. On 8 July 1961 this is the ruinous remains of the stables at the foot of the incline. Maurice Dart.

A short way after the stables Cann Wood Incline commenced and crossed the Plympton to Plym Bridge road on this trestle viaduct seen on 9 January 1926. The GWR's Launceston branch crossed the road a little to the west but is mostly hidden by the LMT structure. The viaduct is extant.

F.H.C Casbourn/Stephenson Locomotive Society.

In the 1930s we look down Cann Wood Incline to the stables. The track is double and is interlaced due to space restrictions with cable rollers and cable present.

In 1922 five wagons of three different sizes loaded with casks of clay are descending self-acting counter-balanced Cann Wood Incline and are about to cross the trestle viaduct. The trackbed of the Cann Quarry branch is on the left. F.H.C. Casbourn/Stephenson Locomotive Society.

This is the top of Cann Wood Incline with its Drumhouse in September 1949. The bridge carried the line over a narrow lane. I was taken along the track from Whitegates level crossing to see 'The Engine House' by my Uncle in 1946. I had expected to see locomotives in the Engine House and was very surprised and puzzled until all was explained to me. Roy Sambourne.

In July 1961 some sections of the track had been lifted but Whitegates level crossing was still guarded by this rudimentary signal. Roy Sambourne.

In May 1948 the gates are closed across the track at Whitegates level crossing which carried the line across the road from Plympton to Shaugh Prior. This view looks towards Cann Wood. Roy Sambourne.

Around 500yd east of Whitegates level crossing the line enters a cutting and passes under Truelove Bridge which carries a narrow minor road. In May 1948 the bridge is in the distance as we head towards Lee Moor. The area around the bridge is quite moist and a little boggy and is known as 'The Ruts'. Originally a 66yd tunnel was proposed here. Roy Sambourne.

From Truelove Bridge the line ran past Coldstone and approached Torycombe to do which it crossed the 205yd Lower Lee viaduct. With a maximum height of around 70ft it was constructed with fifteen spans instead of seventeen as planned. The viaduct was poorly built and tended to be unstable so in 1878 a new route was opened around the side of the valley of the Tory Brook. Most of the viaduct was dismantled but the base of a couple of the fan arches survive but are buried under part of Portworthy Mica Dam. However the west end abutment remains and was recorded on 14 April 1993. Maurice Dart.

In May 1948 several wagons stood on the deviation line which was known as 'The Wotter Curve'.
Roy Sambourne.

After the curve the line ran straight into Torycombe, passing through a gate and over a weighbridge where rails remained in June 1955. Maurice Dart/Transport Treasury.

As the line entered Torycombe it split into two and the line on the right threw off several sidings. In the 1930s 0-4-0ST 'LEE MOOR No.2' (P784/1899) is on a spur which served the calciner. English China Clays.

Before the Calciner was reached a long siding went off on the right and descended to serve two china clay kilns. In the 1930s a solitary wagon is at the back end of the siding that served Great Eastern kiln. The right hand line served Cholwichtown kiln. English China Clays.

The siding that served Cholwichtown kiln continued past it. A line of abandoned wagons stand on the east end of the siding in the late 1940s. Mike Daly.

At Torycombe a siding off the left hand line served Klondyke china clay kiln where wagons and two water ballast wagons are in the 1920s. The ballast wagons were used for working the self-acting counter-balanced Torycombe incline. Mr.Lillicrap/Transport Treasury.

Other sidings from the left hand line served a fitters' shop and Torycmbe loco shed. This is the shed with both locos ensconced in May 1955. Maurice Dart/Transport Treasury.

Photography inside the loco shed was difficult owing to the confined surroundings. On my second day at work, 19 May 1953 0-4-0ST 'LEE MOOR No.1' (P783/1899) is at the rear of the small shed.
Maurice Dart/Transport Treasury.

On 19 May 1953 0-4-0ST 'LEE MOOR No.2' (P784/1899) was at the front end of the loco shed.
Maurice Dart/Transport Treasury.

Both of the lines crossed the road from Plympton to Lee Moor at the ungated Torycombe level crossing. A siding also crossed it to serve Mica kiln. Before the level crossing this siding used to hold wagons was recorded in May 1955. The crossing was controlled by Torycombe Signal Box which is in this photo. A decrepit signal is visible above the wagons. A building on the distant left hillside housed Kelly's Winder which worked an inclined sand tramway which rose up from the Torycombe Valley. Maurice Dart/Transport Treasury.

In the early 1920s 0-4-0ST 'LEE MOOR No.2' (P784/1899) with wagons from the brickworks has stopped on Torycombe level crossing. English China Clays.

In the early 1920s 0-4-0ST 'LEE MOOR No.1' (P783/1899) takes a train from the brickworks over Torycombe level crossing. F.H.C.Casbourn/Stephenson Locomotive Society.

In June 1955 this wagon was the furthest east from Torycombe level crossing, deep inside the brickworks. Various types of brick kilns are visible. The sand tip and Muscovite Plant are in the background.

Maurice Dart/Transport Treasury.

This is an overview of Torycombe brickworks in the early 1920s. Two lines with connecting spurs served various brick kilns. The massive Hoffmann brick kiln is in the right background. English China Clays.

Originally the route from Torycombe to Lee Moor village ran from the centre of the brickworks up the Old Torycombe incline to Blackalder Tor. This incline rose 300ft in 649yd and had a sharply banked curve with negative superelevation at its foot. Several derailments occurred on the curve. The old incline only operated for around six months in 1856 after which there was no connection to the village until September 1858 when the New Torycombe incline opened. At roughly its mid-point the old incline passed through a spoil tip from an adjacent quarry. This shot looks down the incline through the stone wall lined cutting on 14 April 1993. Maurice Dart/Transport Treasury.

The New Torycombe incline rose 715yd to a point several yards west of Blackalder Tor. This is the trackless New Torycombe incline from about one-third of the way up in August 1955.

Maurice Dart/Transport Treasury.

At the summit of the New Torycombe incline the Wotter Tramway made a trailing connection. In 1930 the Wotter line laid on stone blocks is on the left with the line coming up the incline on the right with cables and rollers. The drumhouse is on the left. The small circular building contained steps which led below to the cable drums and the incline man's lookout and bell tower is on the right. These two buildings are extant but the drum pit has been filled in. One of the incline water ballast wagons is beyond the drumhouse.
Stephenson Locomotive Society.

In July 1955 Stone setts remained in abundance approaching 'First Style' on the line to Wotter which closed in 1900. Wotter pit and its associated sand tips form a backdrop. Maurice Dart/Transport Treasury.

Further west the Wotter line crossed the old parish road from Torycombe to Highboro'. Stone setts were partly buried at the crossing in July 1955. Wotter pit tip is in the background. Maurice Dart.

From the top of the incline the line ran to and through Lee Moor village where the clay company's workshops and stores were situated. With Lee Moor and Whitehill Yeo pit's sand tips in the background this busy scene from the early 1900s contains wagons, horses, wagon wheels and piles of logs. One of the buildings contained a blacksmith's shop where horses were shod.

After curving through Lee Moor village the line headed east on an embankment and passed Lee Moor old power station. In July 1955 the trackbed of a siding used to deliver coal is in the cutting passing below a bridge. The main line embankment is on the left. This building still stands.

Maurice Dart/Transport Treasury.

A short distance beyond the old power station the line passed Whitehill Yeo Pit Tip winder. This is the winder in July 1955 with the main route running on a fence-lined embankment behind the building. A siding, used to deliver coal, climbed up to the right to join the main route.

Maurice Dart/Transport Treasury.

The line continued running north-east and crossed the road from Lee Moor to Cornwood at Tolchmoor Gate. It terminated alongside Cholwichtown (locally pronounced Challistun) kilns seen from over the crossing on 11 May 1961. Roy Sambourne/Transport Treasury.

3

PLYMOUTH AREA INDUSTRIAL LOCATIONS

BURRATOR RESERVOIR

A large reservoir to supply Plymouth, Devonport and Stonehouse was constructed at Burrator east of Yelverton in the 1890s. This interesting photo dating from that period has what appears to be standard gauge railway track in the foreground which was used during the construction. Two large steam cranes working on different levels appear to be mounted on small diameter flanged wheels running on rails.

DEVONPORT DOCKYARD

A horse worked tramway existed in the dockyard which opened in 1691. In 1867 it was superseded by a standard gauge line which linked the three sections of the complex and passed through three tunnels in the process. A variety of locos have worked in the dockyard.

In the early 1950s 0-4-0ST No.2 (AB 2221/1946) shunts in North Yard. This loco had previously been known as No.19 but did not carry the number. This engine is preserved on the Dean Forest Railway. Mike Daly.

0-4-0ST No.8 (HL 2821/1910) stands by the Transit shed in South Yard in the early 1950s. This loco was scrapped in 1955. Mike Daly.

In the early 1950s 0-4-0ST No.9 (AB 1406/1915) shunts in North Yard. This engine which came to Devonport from Rosyth was scrapped in 1957. Mike Daly.

The loco shed in South Yard was built with a high roof in order to accommodate steam cranes. In the early 1950s 0-4-0ST No.11 (AB 1380/1914) rests inside the shed. This loco was scrapped in 1957. Note the large blocks fitted around the front buffers.
Mike Daly.

In the early 1950s 0-4-0ST No.12 (AE1690/1915) is at work in Morice Yard which was between North and South Yards. In 1957 this loco was adapted for use as a stationary boiler and was scrapped in 1959. Mike Daly.

0-4-0ST No.13 (AB 1397/1915) stands in North Yard near St Leven Gate in the early 1950s. This loco was scrapped early in 1959. Mike Daly.

Shunting in North Yard in the early 1950s is 0-4-0ST No.14 (HL 3200/1916) which was scrapped during 1957. Mike Daly.

In the early 1950s 0-4-0ST No.15 (HL 3201/1916) runs 'light engine' at North Yard. This loco was scrapped in 1957. Mike Daly.

This is the loco shed at North Yard in the early 1950s. From the right the locos, which are all 0-4-0STs, are No.12 (AE1690/1915), No.13(AB 1397/1915) and No.17 (AB 2071/1939). This last loco was sold to a dealer and was finally scrapped in 1968. Mike Daly.

On 26 January 1963 0-4-0ST No.18 (AB 2137/1942) moves around North Yard near St Leven Gate. This loco was also sold to a dealer and was scrapped during 1968. Peter Gray.

This group of photos ends with North Yard loco shed in the mid-1950s which is occupied by Diesel locos. Outside are two 0-4-0STs, the nearest being No.19 (WB 2962/1950) which is based at the Bodmin & Wenford Railway. An unidentified Andrew Barclay is to its rear. Mike Daly

DEWERSTONE QUARRY TRAMWAY

North of Shaugh tunnel an uncompleted bridge was planned to carry a standard gauge line across the River Mewy, from where it climbed to a loading wharf. From the loading wharf a tramway, believed to be of 2ft gauge climbed for 400yd on a counterbalanced incline graded at 1 in 6 to a reversing point. From the reversing point a line ran south to the main Dewerstone Quarry. The line was around a mile long and worked for around twenty years from 1858. This is the remains of the cable drums in 1926. Stephenson Locomotive Society.

EFFORD FORT TRAMWAY, PLYMOUTH

Manually worked lines of 2ft gauge were laid at the fort in the Second World War when it was used as a supply base. The tracks ran beside lines of casemates and corners were negotiated using small turntables. These three photos were taken during a visit to the fort on 7 April 2004. A line from the fort's yard crosses from the right corner and once connected with the two lines running to the right by the Casemates. A turntable was partly visible in the grassy area on the left. Maurice Dart.

This is one end of the line beside the casemates. Maurice Dart.

The right hand line in the casemates ended at a turntable from which this line turned off right and climbed through a tunnel to reach storage areas on the upper level. Maurice Dart.

ERNESETTLE RNAD RAILWAY. PLYMOUTH

A network of 2ft 6in gauge lines linked storage tunnels to exchange sidings and an Admiralty pier. Early one evening in the late 1950s three narrow gauge diesel locos were on the pier as an Up train crossed the Royal Albert Bridge which formed an excellent photographic vantage point. Mike Daly.

ESSO BITUMEN, CATTEDOWN, PLYMOUTH

This depot was served by standard gauge sidings, one of which curved through a limited clearance tunnel to access a fuel storage site. On 25 October 1971 204HP 0-6-0DM D2134 exits the site. Maurice Dart.

At the bitumen sidings on 23 July 1997 4wDH S 10199/1964 was out of use with a faulty starter. Maurice Dart.

On 23 July 1997 0-6-0DH HC D1373/1965 is coupled to tank wagons which have been loaded with hot liquid bitumen. Maurice Dart.

0-6-0DH HC D1373/1965 takes loaded bitumen tank wagons from the depot to join the Cattewater branch on 23 July 1997. The Cattewater branch skirts the west bank of the River Plym. Maurice Dart.

MARSH MILLS CHINA CLAY DRYERS BRANCH. PLYMOUTH

The Works was connected to Tavistock Junction yard by a sharp curve after which the line passed over two level crossings. From there the line climbed an incline graded at 1 in 50 which steepens to around 1 in 35 up to the

Works. A trap siding was situated half way down the incline as a safety measure. The Works were shunted by GWR locos until English China Clays obtained a loco in 1948, since when several locos have worked there. From early 1991 BR Diesel Shunters took the work over. Around 16.20 on 12 February 2008 09101 'IVOR' brings a second rake of empty CDA wagons around the curve from Tavistock Junction yard towards Marsh Mills No.1 level crossing. Maurice Dart.

09101 'IVOR' takes empty CDA wagons over Marsh Mills No.1 level crossing on 12 February 2008.
Maurice Dart.

On 29 October 2005 08405 brings loaded CDA wagons over Marsh Mills No.1 level crossing. Maurice Dart.

Loaded CDA wagons hauled by 08405 pass the site of Marsh Mills station as they approach Marsh Mills No.1 level crossing on 29 October 2005. Maurice Dart.

Around 15.40 on 4 March 2008 09101 'IVOR' brings loaded CDA wagons over Marsh Mills No.2 level crossing. Maurice Dart.

On 12 February 2008 09101 'IVOR' descends the incline with loaded CDA wagons and approaches Marsh Mills No.2 level crossing. Maurice Dart.

On 20 June 2003 09013 prepares to descend the incline with two loaded Polybulk wagons. Maurice Dart.

09016 'THE SNIPER' approaches the top of the incline with loaded CDA wagons on 4 August 2003.
Maurice Dart.

On 4 March 2008 09101 'IVOR' shunts loaded CDA wagons in the extensive sidings at the Works. Maurice Dart.

09101'IVOR' positions CDA wagons in one of the covered loading areas on 4 March 2008. Maurice Dart.

On 29 October 2005 08405 is positioning CDA wagons for loading.

08405 moves loaded CDA wagons over the weighbridge on 29 October 2005. Maurice Dart.

On 23 July 1997 09013 slowly positions CDA wagons for loading. Maurice Dart.

CDA wagons are being positioned for loading by 09101 'IVOR' on 12 February 2008. Maurice Dart.

On 4 March 2008 09101'IVOR' is shunting CDA wagons at the north end of the complex where four storage sidings form a convenient Headshunt. Maurice Dart.

The is the first loco that was obtained by ECC to work at Marsh Mills. On 15 June 1957 0-4-0DM JF 22917/1940 is stabled beside the coal fired power station. A short string of wagons containing coal stand on the siding.
Maurice Dart/Transport Treasury.

The next loco obtained by ECC was this Fireless engine which was supplied by steam from the power station. On 9 August 1967 0-4-0F WB 3121/1957 is connected to the charging point at the top of the incline. This loco is awaiting restoration at the Bodmin & Wenford Railway.

Maurice Dart/Transport Treasury.

The successor to the Fireless loco was this machine. On 25 September 1988 0-4-0DH EEV 3987/1970 stands over an Inspection Pit. This loco was transferred to Moorswater and later to Broadlands Quarry, Quidhampton near Salisbury. Maurice Dart.

The EEV diesel had been superseded by ex BR 08398 which had been transferred from Fowey, which is stabled partly under cover on 25 September 1988. At this time this loco did not carry any identification. It has since worked at Blackpool and Rocks Dryers but suffered 'Shifted Cranks' in December 2008. Maurice Dart.

MOUNT BATTEN SEAPLANE BASE. PLYMOUTH

For a while when the base was operational a railway line of unknown gauge ran in the site. Cranes ran along it on the pier being used to hoist sea planes to and from the water. This photo from 1917 shows part of the line at RNAS Cattewater. Gerald Wasley Collection.

SHAUGH IRON MINE TRAMWAY

An obscure line, believed to be of 2ft gauge ran from the mine, situated south east of Shaugh Bridge partly beside the river to near a point where the road to Bickleigh crossed the river on a bridge. The line worked from around 1860 for ten years. This old postcard shows the line with possibly rails and sleepers 'in situ' heading south along the east bank of the river.

VICTORIA WHARVES PLYMOUTH

This location was used by Coast Lines for many years and ended up owned by the Escombe Group. Several standard gauge locos have worked here over the years. In the 1920s 0-4-0ST 'ALICIE' (HE 366/1886) shunts the wharves. This loco was rebuilt as an 0-6-0ST. Victoria Wharves Archive.

In the summer of 1956 this Howard 4wPM was stabled on the wharves and two Planet 4wPM locos were inside the dead ended tunnel which served as a loco shed. Mike Daly.

The last loco to work at the wharves was 4wDM FH 3281/1948 which is inside the dead ended tunnel on 6 June 1970. This loco is preserved on the Plym Valley Railway. Maurice Dart.

4

MORWELLHAM QUAY

Narrow gauge lines were operating on the surface at Devon Great Consols mine in 1856. Two years later they were replaced by standard gauge lines and extended for 4½ miles to Morwellham Quay. A self-acting incline took the line on the last section down to the quays. There were several branch lines one of which passed through a short tunnel. The mine ceased operations in 1901 and most track had been removed by 1903. From 1970 renovation work has been ongoing at Morwellham Quays. A 2ft gauge line opened early in 1978 was extended through the George & Charlotte mine for around half a mile to New Quay six months later. On 18 June 2006 loading staithes carrying rails await completion around Devon Great Consols Quay. Several wagons including one loaded with timber are near the dock. Maurice Dart.

On the Devon Great Consols Quay on 18 June 2006 a standard gauge ore wagon sits on rails on partly constructed staithes. Maurice Dart.

Another branch of the Devon Great Consols Mine line ran south on a ledge above the River Tamar. From the ledge chutes took ore from wagons down to be loaded on to waiting boats. On 6 August 2006 I recorded the outlets of five chutes as I approached Morwellham on a boat from Plymouth. The ledge where the railway ran is prominent. Maurice Dart.

A few standard gauge lines remained laid on the surface of the quays on 24 July 2006. This line ran to the lower copper quay. Maurice Dart.

Two 0-4-0Ts built by Gilkes, Wilson operated on the Devon Great Consols Railway. One of these, believed to be (GW 131/1859) is at Wheal Emma, Devon Great Consols. This loco worked until its boiler was worn out in 1886. This painting by Nick Luff was exhibited at Morwellham on 24 July 2006. Maurice Dart.

Two 0-4-0STs also worked on the Devon Great Consols line. Here is 'ADA' (Spittle 5/c1896) at Wheal Josiah, Devon Great Consols. It later worked at Flanders during the First World War. This is from a water colour by Nick Luff.

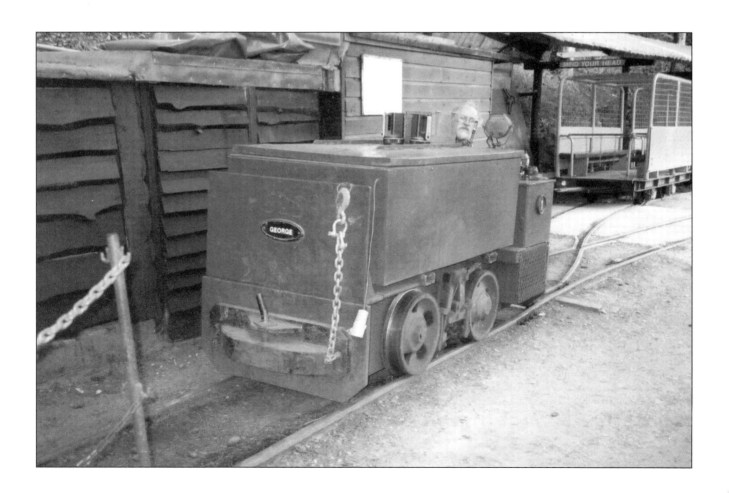

The 2ft gauge line at Morwellham is operated by battery electric locos which take visitors for a ride through the mine and operate maintenance trains. On 18 June 2006 4wBE No.1 'GEORGE' (WR H7197/1968) has uncoupled from the last train of the day and is moving to the charging point. Maurice Dart

Some locos attached to carriages are kept on a loop line immediately south of the terminus at Morwellham. On 24 July 2006 4wBE No.3 'CHARLOTTE' (WR G7124/1967 is stabled on the loop. Maurice Dart.

Stabled on the loop at Morwellham on 24 July 2006 is 4wBE No.7 'HAREWOOD' (WR D6800/1964) with 'CHARLOTTE' to its rear. Maurice Dart.

On 24 July 2006 4wBE No.2 'BERTHA' (WR 6298/1960) approaches Morwellham terminus as it passes locos and stock stabled on the loop. Maurice Dart.

0-4-0BE 'MEX' (WR) which was owned by the Engineer is at Morwellham terminus on 24 September 1988. This loco was not normally used to work passenger trains. Maurice Dart.

On 6 May 2007 4wBE No.5 'WILLIAM' (WR C6770/1964) takes a train from Morwellham into the George & Charlotte mine. Maurice Dart.

This is the Morwellham entrance to the George & Charlotte mine on 6 May 2007. Maurice Dart.

Trains return from New Quay on a line which runs outside the George & Charlotte mine and skirts the river on its bank. That route also happens to be a public footpath. Providing the office is notified first permission can be obtained to walk along the route. On 6 May 2007 4wBE No.5 'WILLIAM' brings a train from New Quay past the Morwellham entrance to the mine. Maurice Dart.

On 6 May 2007 4wBE No.5 'WILLIAM' approaches the entrance to the mine with a train from Morwellham. Maurice Dart.

This is the New Quay entrance to the George & Charlotte mine on 6 May 2007. Maurice Dart.

On 6 May 2007 4wBE No.5 'WILLIAM' leaves the mine with a train for New Quay. Maurice Dart.

This old steam boiler with a very antiquated cowl to its chimney was photographed at New Quay on 6 May 2007. It is believed to have come from a Cornish china clay works. Maurice Dart.

Various items of Engineer's stock was stabled at New Quay on 24 July 2006. Maurice Dart.

On 6 May 2007 4wBE 'HAREWOOD' is in the Engineer's sidings at New Quay. Maurice Dart.

Unusually a locomotive was overhauled and tested at Morwellham for another preservation site. On 24 July 2006 4wP (L 11410/1939) is at New Quay in the Engineer's sidings. It departed early in the following year to the Phoenix Light Railway Trust at Seven Stones Halt near Callington.

Maurice Dart.

On 24 July 2006 4wBE No.4 'LUDO' (WR 6769/1964) departs from New Quay with a train for Morwellham. In the Engineer's sidings is 4wBE No.6 'MARY' (WR 5665/1957). Maurice Dart.

The 2ft gauge line ends just north of New Quay. A rough track descends a bank from the railway and runs south to the abandoned village. It passes through this bridge which carried a tramway used to carry stone from boats on the river to the top of a lime kiln. The large kiln still remains beyond the bridge. On the hillside above on 24 July 2006 is the slightly leaning chimney of Gawton Flue. Gawton mine produced copper, tin, arsenic and iron. Maurice Dart.

5

TAMAR BELLE HERITAGE GROUP BERE FERRERS STATION

A small site to preserve the railways and industrial history of the Tamar Valley was established here in 1991. standard gauge rails have been laid in the station Goods yard and sidings sites. On 15 September 2000 the working locomotive RO70 0-4-0DM (HE 2642/1941) is at the site's platform. The Tamar Valley line is behind the railings on the right. Maurice Dart.

0-4-0DM 'ARMY 54' (HE 3395/1946) is undergoing restoration on 15 September 2000. Maurice Dart.

On 4 March 2008 0-4-0DM (HE 3133/1944) was on display in the yard. This loco previously worked on the Bodmin & Wenford Railway and was named 'LUCY'. Maurice Dart.

Awaiting completion of its restoration on 6 May 2007 is 0-4-0ST (P 1963/1938). Maurice Dart.

6

LYNTON & BARNSTAPLE RAILWAY (RE-OPENED) & LYNBARN RAILWAY

This is the Goods shed at the east end of Lynton station on 9 September 2005. It has been converted to a private residence. Maurice Dart.

The station at Lynton has also been converted for use as a private residence as seen on 9 September 2005. Note the Southern Railway sign to the bottom left of the window. The end of the Goods shed is visible to the left of the hoarding bearing the 'FOR SALE' sign. Maurice Dart.

The 'Station Cat' poses by 2ft gauge 4wDM (RH 179880/1936) on the trackbed alongside the platform at Lynton station on 9 September 2005. Maurice Dart.

The 2ft gauge line terminates at Woody Bay where one line runs east through the loco shed and terminates short of the site of a bridge under the road from Blackmoor Gate to Lynton. On 22 September 2007 4wDM 'TITCH' (MR 8729/1941) is at the end of the line behind items of renovated rolling stock. Maurice Dart.

On 9 September 2005 Hunslet 4wDM 'EXMOOR RANGER' is receiving attention in the locoshed/workshop. This loco carried a plate inscribed 'Vane Tempest. Seaham. 1993'. Maurice Dart.

On very wet 30 December 2006 0-4-0WT 'BRONLLWYD' (HC 1643/1930) is inside the loco shed at midday after working the morning's trains. Maurice Dart.

0-4-0WT 'SID' (Maffei /1925) stands outside the loco shed on 22 September 2007. Maurice Dart.

In heavy rain on 9 September 2005 4wDM 'HOLWELL CASTLE (MR 11177/1961) awaits departure from Woody Bay. The author was treated to a cab ride on this trip. The loco shed is in the background. Maurice Dart.

On 11 September 2004 0-4-0T 'EMMET' has arrived at Woody Bay with an Engineer's train. This loco was Moors Valley Railway No.20 and incorporated parts of an Orenstein & Koppel loco built in 1930. Maurice Dart.

4wDM 'SNAPPER' (RH 283871/1950) stands at Woody Bay on 11 September 2004. Maurice Dart.

On 22 September 2007 0-4-0ST 'STATFOLD' (HE 3903/2005) arrives at Woody Bay on a train from Killington Lane. Maurice Dart.

At Woody Bay a siding climbs south up a gradient ending alongside the station entrance drive. On 9 September 2005 the siding was occupied by a bogie wagon loaded with coal for the locos and a trolley wagon loaded with various items made of wood. Maurice Dart.

On 12 May 2007 0-4-2ST 'STANHOPE' (KS 2395/1917) climbs the bank on the approach to Woody Bay with a train from Killington Lane. The siding to the approach drive is climbing in the foreground. Maurice Dart.

During the very inclement morning of 30 December 2006 0-4-0WT 'BRONLLWYD' is running round its train at Killington Lane. Engineering equipment occupies the sidings. Maurice Dart.

In extremely soggy conditions 0-4-0WT 'BRONLLWYD' is coupling to its train at Killington Lane ready to return uphill to Woody Bay. The low area on the extreme left forms the trackbed to Parracombe. The bridge under Killington Lane requires 'digging out'. Maurice Dart.

Hunslet 4wDM 'HEDDON HALL' is at Killington Lane with a Works train on another miserably wet day on 23 February 2007. On the right the truncated short spur and pile of sleepers are on the trackbed to Parracombe. Maurice Dart.

Beyond Killington Lane the trackbed, now incorporated into fields continues to fall and passed under Parracome Lane where the bridge has been 'filled in'. On 12 May 2007 the parapet of the bridge and top of the stonework forming the arch was extant. Maurice Dart.

The station shelter at Parracombe was 'in situ' with a Post Box affixed to its lower side on 11 May 2007. Maurice Dart.

The trackbed and bridge approaching Blackmoor has been filled in and the station has been transformed into the Old Station House Inn & Restaurant. The 'Signal' was 'Off' inviting us to enter as we look west along the trackbed on 9 September 2005. Inside the building is a large collection of photos and memorabilia relating to the L&B Railway. Hospitality, food and drink are excellent. Maurice Dart.

This is the trackbed looking north from Hennacott, west of Blackmoor on 22 September 2007. Maurice Dart.

Between farms at Hennacott and Narracott around 1067 yards of the trackbed has been transformed into a road linking them. This is a bridge over the trackbed at Narracott where the road has diverged left, seen on 11 May 2005. Maurice Dart.

Various sections of the trackbed are owned either by the railway or by people connected with it. Track sections occupy the trackbed below the bridge east of Bratton Fleming station. From the upper side of this bridge a miniature railway runs down the bank westwards to the station. Its rails are just visible in growth between trees in the upper centre of the photo, taken on 11 September 2004. Maurice Dart.

The railway had a workshop remote from the line around half a mile north east of Bratton Fleming village. On 11 September 2004 it contained 4wDM 'HOLWELL CASTLE' (MR 11177/19610) which was undergoing an overhaul. Use here has ceased. Maurice Dart.

The trackbed around Chelfham station was occupied by stock awaiting restoration on 11 September 2004. The station building is a private residence. West of the station the trackless viaduct has been reconditioned but access across it is barred by gates. Maurice Dart.

The ½ mile long 2ft gauge Lynbarn Railway opened in 1994 at Milky Way Farm Park several miles south of Clovelly. It was intended to contribute profits to the L&B Railway. On 30 October 2004 0-4-0DM 'PARRACOMBE' (Bg 3232/1947) was stabled on the Works line opposite the single platform. Maurice Dart.

Receiving attention at the Works on 30 October 2004 was 4w-4wDM (SL 23/1973) which had previously worked on the Southport Pier Railway. Maurice Dart.

On 30 October 2004 4wDH 'SIR GEORGE' (AK 12/1984) waits at the station to depart for a trip around the circuit. Maurice Dart.

4wDH 'SIR GEORGE' has departed from the station and is about to negotiate the fully signalled and electronically protected level crossing before passing through a short tunnel on 30 October 2004. Maurice Dart.

On 30 October 2004 4wDH 'SIR GEORGE' is halfway around the circuit with a train. Maurice Dart.

7

NORTH, SOUTH & WEST DEVON MILITARY RAILWAYS

OKEHAMPTON BATTLE CAMP RANGES

Four target railways have existed in the area. The earliest, which dates from the time of the Boer War, is called the Okehampton Target Tramway. This 1ft 6in gauge line ran from the east side of East Mill Tor down the side of the moor to the valley of the East Okement River which it crossed by a lightly constructed bridge which still stands. A branch ran towards East Okement Farm. On 14 July 2005 the trackbed, running diagonally from the bottom left corner, crossed the Military Ring Road. From there it ran in a gradually deepening cutting on the right side of the road. The road was not built when the line was constructed. Maurice Dart.

Some track remained in the cutting on 14 July 2005, and also here where the line crossed a small brook.
Maurice Dart.

The next tramway was laid to 2ft 6in gauge around the start of the Second World War. It ran east of West Mill Tor. This is the trackbed which can be seen as a furrow running north-east on 14 July 2005.
Maurice Dart.

Around 1942 the line was taken up and relaid south east of its previous alignment. This line is still extant and is called The Wickham Target Railway or H1. On 20 October 2001 this is the loco shed where the two Wickham trolleys were housed. Maurice Dart.

There is a turning circle at each end of the line and this is the north-west points on 20 October 2001. Maurice Dart.

From the points the line climbed up through a cutting which was partly flooded on 20 October 2001. The track has since been renovated which involved blowing up sections where live ordnance was discovered in the trackbed. Maurice Dart.

This looks north-west along the trackbed on 20 October 2001. Maurice Dart.

The line was out of use for some years and one of the Wickhams went to the Museum of Army Transport at Beverley on closure of which it moved to the Leighton Buzzard Narrow Gauge Railway. The second Wickham went on loan to the Museum of Dartmoor Life in Okehampton where it was stored, partly buried beneath other items, in a yard. In mid-2002 the line

was brought back into use and the Wickham was reclaimed and renovated at the Army's Workshops. On 14 July 2005 767138 'CAPTAIN' (Wkm 3284/1943) was brought outside the shed to be photographed.
Maurice Dart.

Two further Wickhams were obtained from Lydd Ranges in Kent. One was renovated but was found to be out of gauge being 600mm instead of 2ft 6in. The other remained in 'as obtained' condition. On 21 September 2007 767149 'PRESIDENT' (Wkm 3151/1943) and 767163 (Wkm 3236/1943) are in a compound adjacent to the main office near the entrance to the Battle Camp. Maurice Dart.

The fourth line in the area was the 2ft gauge winch-worked Blackdown Target Tramway which dates from 1942. It ran down Blackdown, crossed the Military Ring Road and approached the upper reaches of the Red-a-Ven Brook which is near to its terminal point where the remains of the base of the winch are extant. This looks south along the trackbed towards Blackdown on 14 July 2005. Maurice Dart.

Scattered on the west side of the trackbed near to its terminating point on 14 July 2005 was this selection of pulley wheels mounted on decaying sleepers. Maurice Dart.

WILLSWORTHY RANGES

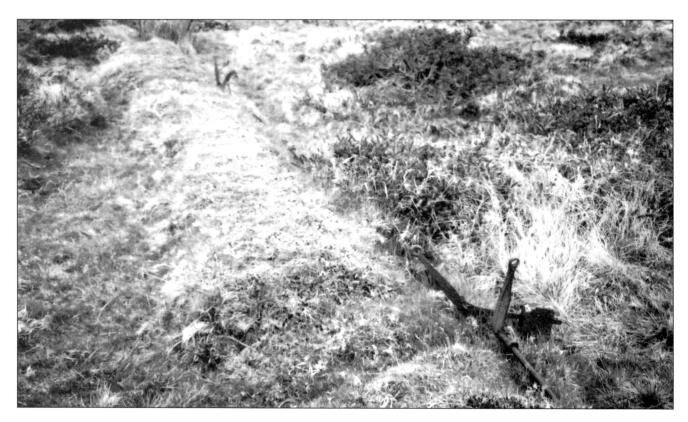

These are situated north-east of the twin villages of Mary Tavy and Peter Tavy. Three lines have existed here but only that to the north-east has any traceable remains. The track on the left was covered in growth on 5 May 2008 but running diagonally from the right lower corner was this line of 'Pop-Up' Target levers. Maurice Dart.

On 5 May 2008 it seemed that most of the track remained 'in situ' albeit mostly covered by growth of various forms. In places rails appear such as here where the line, running north-east, crossed a small gully in the cutting approaching the 'Enclosures'. Maurice Dart.

FROWARD POINT, KINGSWEAR

During the Second World War defences were constructed below cliffs around the point from Kingswear. A 2ft gauge cable-operated line was constructed to take supplies and ammunition down to the batteries. In later years the defences were mostly dismantled but rails remained 'in situ'. This is the base of the winch at the top of the incline on 5 September 1998. One of several storage bunkers is in the background. Maurice Dart.

This looks up the double track incline from around one-third of the way down on 5 September 1998.
Maurice Dart.

The base of some of the mounts for the defences are at the top of this view taken looking down the incline from around its mid-point on 5 September 1998. Growth is encroaching on each of the outside rails.
Maurice Dart.

8

SOUTH WEST & NORTH WEST DEVON INDUSTRIAL LOCATIONS

FATHERFORD TRAMWAY

This horse-worked tramway of uncertain gauge opened in 1870. It ran from Fatherford Quarry south for seven-eighths of a mile and terminated just below Okehampton station. It carried stone from the quarry used in the construction of viaducts and bridges. After construction ceased the quarry and tramway remained in use. Timber was carried on the tramway during the First World War. Rails were finally removed during the 1930s. Despite the rails being retained for many years no photos of the line have come to light. The route is used as footpath and is referred to locally as 'along the old tram lines'. This view looks north on 23 July 1994 from just below Okehampton station.

Maurice Dart.

On 23 July 1994 this view looks north three-quarters of the way along the route to the quarry. Maurice Dart.

MEETH. ECC BALL CLAY WORKS

A long siding connected the processing plant to the national network. A 2ft gauge system ran from the plant to the Ball Clay pits. 2ft gauge 4wDM 237897/1945 is inside one of the loading areas on 20 March 1965.
Roger Hateley.

MELDON VALLEY TRAMWAYS

Industrial sites have operated below Meldon viaduct on both banks of the West Okement River. This view from the early 1900s has a large lime kiln on the west bank of the river. A 2ft gauge tramway ran from the Limestone (Apatite) quarry to the kiln and its rails are on the left at the top of the kiln. The east bank was the site of a Green

Glass Bottle works which also had 2ft gauge lines. In this view a wagon is on a line on the left of one of the works buildings. Another line curves around in front of the building and climbs up a gradient passing through the right hand gate. This line was used to bring supplies down the hillside. A third line which heads towards the bottom right corner ran to the apatite (granulite) quarries.

This is the abutments of a bridge which carried the apatite tramway on the west bank of the river, photographed on 6 August 2000. Maurice Dart.

This is the abutments of another bridge which carried the apatite tramway, 6 August 2000. Maurice Dart.

The apatite tramway on the east bank of the river threw off various sidings to serve different working areas. On 6 August 2000 several trackbeds of these are in the photo with mounds of blackish green Granulite stone adjacent. One of the works buildings is in the mid-distance. Maurice Dart.

RATTLEBROOK PEAT RAILWAY

This standard gauge line dating from 1879 ran from Bridestowe station for seven miles up onto the high moor to Peat works at around the 1000ft contour. Horses provided the motive power. Photos of the line in use have eluded the author. Photographed on an evening of thick rain coupled with Dartmoor mist on 29 June 1998 this is an underline bridge two-thirds of the way along the route. Maurice Dart.

REDLAKE RAILWAY

This 3ft gauge line opened in 1911 and ran for seven miles from the drying kilns at Cantrell, north of Ivybridge up across the moor to China Clay pits at around the 600ft level. Clay was piped to the kiln and the railway carried workers and supplies to the pits. In 1933 0-4-2ST 'DARTMOOR' (KS 1146/1912) is stored together with parts of pumps from the works waiting to be scrapped. Stephenson Locomotive Society.

An incline rose from the kiln to the start of the locomotive worked section across the moor. In 1921 0-4-2T 'C.A.HANSON' (KS 1228/1911) waits near the top of the incline with a train to the clay pits.
Locomotive & General Railway Photographs.

Carriages Nos.4 and 3 await scrapping at Cantrell in 1933. Stephenson Locomotive Society.

Carriage No.1 awaits scrapping at Cantrell in 1933. Stephenson Locomotive Society.

Severe weather is experienced annually on Dartmoor. In November 1921 4wVBT 'LADY MALLABY-DEELEY' (AtW 111/1928) is in a snow drift near the clay pits. The driver, Harry Fox is on the loco and the Works' Superintendent, George Bray is standing alongside.

Locomotive & General Railway Photographs.

This is the dilapidated remains of the loco shed near the top of the incline some time after the line closed. Harold S.A.Fox.

This is the abutments of a bridge over the incline above Cantrell works on 5 March 2008.
Maurice Dart.

TORRINGTON & MARLAND LIGHT
RAILWAY/NORTH DEVON CLAY COMPANY

This 3ft gauge line opened in 1881 ran from Torrington station to Ball clay works on Marland and Merton Moors. In 1925 the first 4 ½ miles of the route were incorporated into the standard gauge North Devon & Cornwall Junction Light Railway along with the branch to the processing works at Peters Marland. 3ft gauge lines connected the works to the clay pits. 3ft gauge 0-6-0ST 11 'AVONSIDE' (AE 1428/1901) is on a train at Watergate on an unknown date.

This four-wheeled coach, recorded on 5 July 1912, was originally a London County Council Horse Tramcar.

This is 0-4-0 'JERSEY 1' (FJ 129/1873) on a train of loaded wagons probably in the 1920s. The line possessed three Fletcher Jenning locos which were originally saddle tanks. They were somewhat heavy for the rather lightly laid track so in 1910 the problem was solved by removing their saddle tanks and placing them on a flat wagon behind the loco to which they were connected by a hose. North Devon Shunter Group.

Around 1920 0-4-0T '3 'PETER' (Lewin /1876) is on a train near the clay pits.

In the 1950s 3ft gauge 4wDM 'FORWARD' (JF 3900012/1947) approaches Marland works with a loaded train from the clay pits. North Devon Shunter Group.

Standard gauge 0-4-0DM (rebuilt as a DH in 1977) (PROGRESS' (JF 4000001/1945) waits to depart from the works with a train to the exchange sidings in the 1950s. This loco spent many years on the Bodmin & Wenford Railway but moved during 2008 to a preservation site at Torrington station. North Devon Shunter Group.

In the 1950s Ball Clay is being transferred from a 3ft gauge wagon to a standard gauge wagon at Marland works. North Devon Shunter Group.

Crushed Ball Clay is being loaded into 3ft gauge wagons at Marland works in the 1950s.
North Devon Shunter Group.

3ft gauge 0-6-0T 'MARLAND' (WB 566/1883) has arrived at Marland works on 11 August 1899 with a train conveying members of the Devonshire Association for a visit to the site. R.Hansford Worth/Bob Cook Collection.

ZEAL TOR TRAMWAY

In 1847 a 'Woodway' was laid to carry peat from works at Redlake Mire to a kiln at Shipley Bridge west of Brent where naptha was extracted. This ceased in 1850 but from 1877 the Brent Moor China Clay works used part of the line for a few years to move supplies. The 5ft gauge line ran for 3 miles. Wooden rails were laid on granite blacks. On 5 March 2008 this is the remains of the kiln at Shipley Bridge. Maurice Dart.

On 5 March 2008 the walls of the holding tanks could be seen on the hillside above the kiln. Bushes and other growth sprout from the tanks. Maurice Dart.

9

LUNDY ISLAND

In 1897 a lighthouse was built on the north west point of Lundy Island. Only a rough track runs from the village to the north tip so to facilitate delivering supplies to the new North Light a 2ft gauge manually worked tramway was laid for several hundred yards from the lighthouse to a point above the sea from where a winch hauled supplies up over a large flat rock. When the lighthouse became automated in 1980 use of the line ceased. On 7 September 2005 the North Light is seen from a vantage point several yards below the end of the island's rough track. The railway runs on the shelf midway down the slope. Maurice Dart.

To reach the railway it was necessary to descend 205 steps, arranged in flights of varying steepness, mostly without any handrail. I was so gratified to see the line at close quarters that I took this shot before I descended the last couple of shallow flights of steps on 7 September 2005. The supports on the right of the line carried the power supply to the winch.
Maurice Dart.

On 7 September 2005 almost all of the rails remained 'in situ' but had come apart in places and one stretch was somewhat boggy. The scenery is spectacular looking along the line towards the winch mounting.
Maurice Dart.

This is the plinth on which the winch was mounted together with adjacent ancillary equipment on 7 September 2005. Maurice Dart.

This is where the line ended on 7 September 2005. The top of the long flat sloping rock up which supplies were winched is in the right lower corner. To access the bottom of that rock it was necessary to descend a further 163 steps at least. Further steps existed below the water line. I abstained from doing so but one member of our small group of three did so and was rewarded with a close up sight of a large seal looking straight at him from the sea. Maurice Dart.

Artist's impression of the quarry whilst in operation. Copyright Jane Breyne

Between 1863 and 1868 five quarries were worked on the east side of the island. A railway, probably of 2ft gauge linked them to a marshalling yard and to Quarry Beach via three inclines. The top quarry was 80ft above the two line marshalling yard from where a line ran north on gradients of 1in 86, 1 in 33, 1 in 14 and 1in 13 to reach the other quarries. Lines from turntables ran into the quarries and to spoil tips on the cliffs. The incline to the top quarry climbed at 1 in 2½ whilst that to Quarry Beach fell at 1 in 1½. I took this photo of a panel in the small Lundy Museum on 7 September 2005. It shows the system as it existed when working. In the foreground is the incline to the beach with winding drums. Above them is the marshalling yard with cutting and storage sheds. Quarries, derrick cranes and spoil tips are in the distance.

Landmark Trust/Maurice Dart.

In this view from 6 September 2005 the marshalling yard, now called 'The Terrace' is centre right with quarries and spoil tips in the distance. The third member of our group, who saw the seal, is standing on one of the inclines, which was crossed by an earlier incline. He later descended a steep path from the north end of 'The Terrace' to the beach where he found little in the way of remains.

Maurice Dart.

On 6 September 2005 this is a close up view of one of the circular granite drum pits at the top of the incline to the beach. Maurice Dart.

On 7 September 2005 this is the granite trough through which the cables passed from the drums to the top of the incline which descends to the left through the foliage. Maurice Dart.

SOUTH EAST & NORTH EAST DEVON INDUSTRIAL LOCATIONS

BOVEY BRICKWORKS

A narrow gauge tramway linked clay pits across the road to a Brickworks and Pottery at Bovey Tracey. It was out of use and blocked in places when I took this photo on 20 June 1965. Maurice Dart.

EXETER GAS WORKS

This system was connected to the GWR by short branch lines from the Teign Valley line and the main line near City Basin Junction. With a large mound of coal as a backdrop 0-4-0ST (P 2031/1942) shunts at the site in November 1963. This loco is preserved on the South Devon Railway at Buckfastleigh.

E.Best/L.Goodman Collection.

With industrial plant nearby 0-4-0ST (P 2074/1946) shunts at the works on 3 February 1962. Richard Murrin.

HEY TOR TRAMWAY

This is the trackbed entering No.2 Quarry on 20 June 1965. Maurice Dart.

This line of 4ft 3in gauge which opened in 1820 ran for seven miles from the Stover Canal at Teignrace to quarries in the area around Hey Tor (modern spelling is Hay Tor). The rails were formed of granite from the quarries. Part of the route was later used by the Moretonhampstead branch line. On 20 June 1965 during a visit by Plymouth Railway Circle this is the junction point of the lines from No.1 and No.2 Quarries. Maurice Dart.

HOLLACOMBE, TORQUAY

The GWR line was doubled between Torquay and Paignton during the Autumn of 1910. This involved opening out 123yd long Livermead (Torquay) tunnel which was also locally called Hollacombe tunnel. In this period 0-6-0ST 'EVELYN' (HC 542/1900) is in use on the work by contractor Robert T. Relf & Son.

PINHOE. DEVON COUNTY COUNCIL CENTRAL VEHICLE & PLANT REPAIR DEPOT

I took this desperate photo from a Down SR express passing at around 80mph on 26 July 1959. Facing the camera almost front end on is 0-4-0ST No.56 'LORNA DOONE' (KS 4250/1922). This loco had worked at Wilminstone quarry, near Tavistock. It is preserved in the Museum of Science & Industry at Birmingham. Maurice Dart.

SIDMOUTH HARBOUR RAILWAY

A 'Woodway' of about 3ft 6in gauge was laid in 1836 from the site of the proposed harbour at Sidmouth. It ran eastwards for 1¼ miles along the esplanade, crossed a viaduct over the River Sid and entered a 1/3rd mile long tunnel which passed through Salcombe Hill Cliff to reach quarries at Hook Ebb. A steam loco was delivered by sea but was too high to pass through the tunnel which only had 6ft headroom. The loco was transported overland and gave tourists rides along the esplanade. The Harbour did not come to fruition. The tunnel was blocked at each end. In December 1994 violent storms combined with heavy seas caused part of the west side of Salcombe Hill Cliff to break away. This revealed the long lost tunnel mouth which I photographed in very high winds on 31 January 1995 whilst on a day out to celebrate my 63rd birthday. The portal was soon blocked up but as this cliff has been collapsing (in May 2009) it may appear again. Maurice Dart.

SILVERTON PAPER MILL

A siding around one-third of a mile long diverged from the Down side of the GWR main line east of Silverton station. I was unaware of this line's existence until a friend who was driving me around stopped her car on the line. The obvious thing to do was to walk along it in each direction. This is near where it joined the main line which is behind the trees on the left. Farm buildings occupied the trackbed on 15 June 1997. All the photos in this section were taken on the same date. Maurice Dart

This is the line shortly after leaving the farm area. The line which was horse worked closed in the 1960s. Maurice Dart.

As the line approached the paper mill area on we discovered a weighbridge between the rails which I photographed looking back towards the junction. Maurice Dart.

Approaching the paper mill the line became double track with a connection between them. The two tracks separated to serve different parts of the complex. Maurice Dart.

The left hand line curved through this loading area but as the premises stopped just beyond I did not follow it through. Also we had not seen anyone to seek permission to investigate further. Maurice Dart.

The right hand line continued past the buildings and curved left to end by offices and another part of the mill. Maurice Dart.

TEIGNMOUTH OLD QAUY

The standard gauge internal lines on the quay were once connected to the GWR main line. A road tractor which could be converted to run on rails was used on the quay for many years along with a steam lorry. In 1956 2-2-0VBT 'THE ELEPHANT' (S 5644/1923) stands among wood stores on the quay.

On 1 August 1959 2-2-0VBT 'THE ELEPHANT' (S 5644/1923) is coupled to a van on the quay. J.Osgood.

PRESTON ROAD GAS WORKS, PAIGNTON

The Gas Works was served by a siding on the Up side of the GWR line between Paignton and Torquay. On 19 May 1957 4wPM converted to DM (RH 402809/1956) was standing on the siding as I passed on a train bound for Kingswear. This loco moved to Exeter Gas works in 1968. The site is sometimes called Hollacombe Gas Works. Maurice Dart.

WESTLEIGH QUARRY, BURLESCOMBE

In 1873 a 3ft gauge line was laid by the Bristol & Exeter Railway from their line at Burlescombe for ¾ of a mile to the quarries. The quarry company took the line over in 1898 and relaid it to standard gauge but retained 3ft gauge track within the quarry. In this interesting photo 0-6-0ST 'CANTREFF' (MW 1235/1893) is on the lower standard gauge line with some dubious looking locally constructed wagons. On a train of Jubilee wagons on the 3ft gauge trestle viaduct is one of the B & E Rly. 0-4-0WTs, either GWR 1381 (built 1873) or 1382 (built 1875). As the Saddle tank arrived after early August 1898 and the Well tanks departed during March 1899 this photo was taken between those dates. English China Clays.

11

LIGHT PASSENGER RAILWAYS & CLIFF RAILWAYS

BABBACOMBE CLIFF RAILWAY, TORQUAY

This line of 5'8" gauge runs down to the beach for 716ft on an average gradient of 1 in 2.83. On a very wet afternoon one of the cars waits at the top station. Both of these photos were taken on 16 April 2004.
Maurice Dart.

One of the cars is beginning its descent.
Maurice Dart.

LYNTON & LYNMOUTH CLIFF RAILWAY

In the 1930s a car is waiting to commence the climb from Lynmouth. Solograph Series.

This 3'9" gauge line drops for 862ft from Lynton to Lynmouth on an average gradient of 1 in 1.75. The cars are fitted with water tanks. The tank on the downward bound car is filled up to lift the upward bound car on the counterbalanced principle. On arrival at the Lynmouth the tank is emptied ready to ascend. In the 1900s a car is approaching Lynmouth. The water tank can be seen below the body of the car. The bodies can be detached to permit a vehicle to be carried. Valentine's Series.

On 11 May 2007 a descending car is about to pass an upward bound car around the halfway point. Maurice Dart.

BIDEFORD, WESTWARD HO & APPLEDORE RAILWAY

This standard gauge line opened the six miles from Bideford to Northam in 1901 and was extended to Appledore on 1908. Closure took place during 1917. On an unknown date 2-4-2T 'KINGSLEY' (HE 714/1900) has arrived at Bideford Quay with a two coach train. Reginald T.Reeves/Exmoor Heritage Postcards.

An unidentified loco on an unknown date in the early 1900s has passed the Kingsley Statue as it approaches Bideford Quay with a train from Westward Ho. Reginald T.Reeves/Exmoor Heritage Postcards.

This is the carriage shed on the outskirts of Bideford on extremely wet 10 May 2007. The building is used by a coach company. Unfortunately the loco shed which adjoined this building has been demolished.
Maurice Dart.

On 10 May 2007 the gate at the entrance to the approach path to Abbotsham Road station remained 'in situ'. Maurice Dart.

On an unknown date 2-4-2T 'KINGSLEY' (HE 714/1900) is on the outskirts of Bideford at Strand Road Halt on a train for Westward Ho. Reginald T.Reeves/Exmoor Heritage Postcards.

One of the 2-4-2Ts is stopped at Westward Ho station on a train bound for Appledore. It has passed a train bound for Bideford on an unknown date in the early 1900s. Two of the three locos were loaded onto a boat bound for war service in Europe. Unfortunately the ship was torpedoed off the North Cornish coast and sank. The locos remain on the sea bed to this day. Impending salvage attempts have been rumoured.
Reginald T.Reeves/Exmoor Heritage Postcards.

This is the remains of Appledore station and platform on very wet 10 May 2007. A tablet mounted on the wall depicts the chassis of a 2-4-2T with APPLEDORE STATION above it. Maurice Dart.

12

PRESERVATION SITES

BICTON WOODLAND RAILWAY

This 1ft 6in gauge line runs through the grounds of Bicton Park for around 1000yd. There are three stations, one of which is accessed by a triangular junction. On 4 January 2007 a train at the Bicton terminus waits to depart behind 0-4-0DH 'SIR WALTER RALEIGH' (AK 61/2000). In the background on a siding is 4wDM 'CLINTON' (HE 2290/1941).

Maurice Dart.

BIDEFORD STATION

The Bideford Railway Co. have established a small preservation site at the old station since 2000. On wet 10 May 2007 standard gauge 4wDM (FH 3832/1957) was present at the site.

Maurice Dart.

DARTMOOR RAILWAY/AGGREGATE INDUSTRIES

This is the standard gauge line from Yeoford to Meldon Quarry. During an experimental 'Folk Train' on 2 September 2000 local band 'Walter Shortage & Hosepipe Banned' play alongside 0-4-0DH 'FLYING FALCON' (JF 4220022/1962) at Meldon Quarry terminus. The viaduct is hidden by the loco and carriage. Maurice Dart.

A variety of locomotives and rolling stock have been stabled in the extensive sidings at Meldon Quarry where 'Secure Storage' is available. On very wintery 29 December 2005 during a heavy snow shower 47716 is stabled on a rake of carriages. Alongside the brick loco shed is psuedo class 08 shunter ex Netherlands Railway NS 663. The short siding on the right holds Wickham trolley RLC/009023 003 (WKM 8087/1958) which is owned by RMS Locotec Ltd. Maurice Dart.

On 5 May 2008 the Dartmoor Railway's regular shunter (08937 but now un-numbered) 'BLUEBELL MEL' was back at Meldon Quarry after being overhauled. In the foreground is the cab of 0-6-0T ('FIREFLY') (HC 1864/1952) which was previously ensconced at Colwyn Bay station. Maurice Dart.

DEVON RAILWAY CENTRE, CADLEIGH STATION, BICKLEIGH BRIDGE

An Industrial Railway Museum has been established at this site since 1997. A varied collection of mainly 2ft gauge locos are present along with a 2ft gauge running line and miniature railways. A standard gauge diesel loco is on site together with carriages which contain interesting model railway layouts of Industrial locations. On 2 August 2008 0-4-0BE 'S14 1300' (WR /c1950) was on static display with two Jubilee wagons.
Maurice Dart.

On static display with a type of skip wagon on 2 August 2008 was 4wDM 'CLAUDE' (RH 435398/1959) which worked at the North Devon Clay Co. at Peters Marland, after which it had a spell on the Seaton Tramway where it was regauged from 3ft to 2ft 9in.
Maurice Dart.

Two locos on static display on 9 December 2006 were 4wDH (MR 105H006/1969) which had been regauged from 3ft and 4wDM (FH 2201/1939). Maurice Dart.

Two 2ft gauge locos on display on 19 December 1999 were 4wDH 'MERLIN' (HU HX1001/1968) and 4wDM (RH 235711/1945). 'MERLIN' departed in 2001. In the background is standard gauge 0-4-0DM 'BORIS' (Bg 3357/1952). Maurice Dart.

On static display on 9 December 2006 were 4wDM 'SIR TOM' (MR 40S273/1966) and standard gauge 0-4-0DM 'BORIS'. In the left foreground is the front of 0-4-0ST 'PIXIE' (KS 4260/1922) which was operating trains on the 2ft gauge line. Maurice Dart.

On 19 December 1999 in the background is standard gauge 0-4-0DM 'BORIS' (Bg 3357/1952). In the foreground is 4wPM 6299 (L 6299/1935). Maurice Dart.

Trains were being worked by 4wDM 'IVOR' (MR 8877/1944) on 19 December 1999. The building on the right is the locomotive shed and Museum. Maurice Dart.

On 2 August 2008 inside the loco shed was the boiler off 0-4-0WT (OK 5744/1912) which is undergoing an overhaul. When completed the loco may be named 'REBECCA'. Maurice Dart.

Several locos are stored out of use behind the loco shed awaiting refurbishment. On 9 December 2006 4wDM (FH 1747/1931) was partly sheeted over for protection from the elements. Maurice Dart.

On 9 December 2006 this line up behind the loco shed comprised, from the left, 4wDM (L 34025/1949) against which the cab of the 0-4-0WT (5744/1912) is resting. In front is completely sheeted over 4wDM (FH 2025/1937). Maurice Dart.

At the north-east end of the shed yard on 9 December 2006 was 4wDM (MR 20073/1950). Maurice Dart.

On 2 August 2007 0-4-0ST 'PIXIE' (KS 4260/1922) is running round its train. On the left is 4wDM (RH 418770/1957). Maurice Dart.

On 2 August 2008 alternate trains were double headed. The next to last train of the day is halfway round the line hauled by 0-4-0ST 'PIXIE' (KS 4260/1922) and visiting 0-4-0ST 'PETER PAN' (KS 4256/1922). Maurice Dart.

When the last public run ended on 2 August 2008 the two 0-4-0STs were facing in opposite directions. The owner Matthew Gicquel, drove one loco around the line to reverse the direction in which it faced and arranged for the locos to be lined up outside the shed for the author to photograph. From the left they are 0-4-0ST 'PIXIE', 0-4-0ST 'PETER PAN' and 4wDM 'HORATIO' (RH 217967/942) which carries an 81S shedplate. Maurice Dart.

EXETER & TEIGN VALLEY RAILWAY. CHRISTOW STATION

A preservation site was established at the site of Christow station about 1993. Standard and narrow gauge items are present. On 17 June 2000 0-4-0DM ('PERSEUS') (VF D98/1949/DC 2269/1949) is attached to a van and a GWR Toad Brake van. To the upper right of centre in the background is a small manually propelled narrow gauge riding vehicle. Various narrow gauge wagons are present. Maurice Dart

On 17 June 2000 during a visit by Plymouth Railway Circle rides were available in this 4wDM PW railcar DR 90011. Maurice Dart.

Also present on 17 June 2000 was Wickham PW Trolley PWM 2831 (WKM 5009/1949). Maurice Dart.

When the site was visited on very wet 31 July 2008 the Wickham Trolley was undergoing a long term overhaul in the well equipped workshop. Maurice Dart.

EXMOOR STEAM RAILWAY, NEAR BLACKMOOR GATE

Narrow gauge locos of various gauges are built here by the Stirland family. In the 1990s public rides were available on a 1ft 3in gauge line which was about a mile in length. In the mid-1990s the gauge was altered to 12 1/2in. Passengers ceased to be carried in 2004 and the site is closed to the public. The line is maintained as a 'Test Track' for locos constructed for various buyers including some overseas. On 10 May 2007 0-4-2T 'LORNA DOONE' (Works No.191) is at Exmoor Town station with sheeted over carriages. Maurice Dart.

Stabled adjacent to 'LORNA DOONE' on 10 May 2007 is 0-4-2T 'DENZIL'. Maurice Dart.

The workshop adjoins the platform at Exmoor Town station. On the stabling road in the late 1990s is 2-8-0T 'YEO VALLEY. (Works No.190).

Stabled at the back end of the platform on 23 February 2007 is 2ft gauge 4wDH 92.001 (HE 9333/1994). Maurice Dart.

In the workshop on 21 September 2007 2ft gauge 4wDH (HE 9336/1994) is looking a bit the worse for wear. Maurice Dart.

In another building completed 7 1/4in gauge 0-4-2T 'JILLIE' was hiding in a corner on 10 May 2007. Maurice Dart.

On a different gauge trolley in the Erecting Shop on 10 May 2007 is a partly completed 7 1/4in gauge 0-4-2T.
Maurice Dart.

On 10 May 2007 this 10 1/4in gauge 0-4-2T is partly complete in the Erecting Shop. Maurice Dart.

On 21 September 2007 12 1/4in gauge 0-4-2T 'VICTORIA' (332/2007) sits on a trolley wagon, almost complete in the Erecting shop. A pair of 7 1/4in gauge 0-4-2Ts are in the background. Maurice Dart.

A 10 1/4in gauge 2-4-2T is on a trolley wagon in front of a 12 1/4in gauge 2-6-2 which is on track in the Erecting shop on 10 May 2007. Maurice Dart.

The 12 1/4in gauge 2-6-2 was nearing completion in the Erecting shop on 21 September 2007. Maurice Dart.

In another section of the Erecting shop on 21 September 2007 is this 2ft gauge 2-6-0. This 'Rolling Chassis' was built in South Africa and arrived here in June 2003. Maurice Dart.

During my visit on 10 May 2007 I was surprised to be shown a pair of 7 1/4in gauge 0-4-2Ts which were stored partly completed side by side in an additional elevated storage area in the Erecting shop. Space is at a premium. Maurice Dart.

Stored inside a separate building on 10 May 2007 is this partly constructed 12 1/4in gauge 0-4-0 + 0-4-0T. Photography was difficult in this confined area. Maurice Dart.

On 23 February 2007 a storage area which adjoins the Erecting shop contained ex SAR Garratt 2-6-2T + 2-6-2T 77 which arrived from the Brecon Mountain Railway. Several Steam Rollers were present. Maurice Dart.

Photographed through the fence, three ex SAR Garratts, all 2-6-2 + 2-6-2Ts, in the yard on 29 August 1999 are 87, 130 and 115. I was very surprised to find these locos at this location. The nearest loco, 87 is working on the Welsh Highland Railway. Maurice Dart.

At the end of a line of locos in the yard on 21 September 2007 is ex SAR Garratt 2-6-2 + 2-6-2T 130.
Maurice Dart.

The centre loco in the line in the yard on 21 September 2007 is ex SAR Garratt 2-6-2 + 2-6-2T 115.
Maurice Dart.

At the lower end of the line of locos in the yard on 21 September 2007 is ex SAR 2-8-2 135. Unfortunately there is no tender with this loco. Maurice Dart.

At the bottom end of the yard in thick rain on 10 May 2007 is ex SAR Garratt 2-6-2 + 2-6-2T 109. Maurice Dart.

Running round its train at Cape of Good Hope Halt on 29 August 1998 is 12 1/4in gauge 0-4-2T 'DENZIL'.

Maurice Dart.

POWDERHAM CASTLE RAILWAY

A 1ft 3in gauge line ran for around 1/3rd of a mile from near the entrance to the castle to a remote part of the surrounding grounds. It opened in August 2001 but due to continuing problems with the locomotive it closed early in 2003. When I visited and when I made other enquiries later, the line was always out of action. I had to be satisfied by walking the track and viewing the loco through the shed windows! Luckily a friend who visited the site on 7 April 2002 found replica GWR Dukedog 3205 'EARL OF DEVON' working and took this photograph as the train arrived at the Old Smithy terminus. A platform under construction on the right of the train was never completed. Simon Mortimer.

INDEX